A LOVE REMEMBERED
IS A LOVE FOREVER

ONE MAN'S TRIBUTE TO A WOMAN HE CANNOT FORGET

ROBERT ALAN GLOVER

Published by Robert Alan Glover

Copyright 2016 by Robert Alan Glover

A Love Remembered Is a Love Forever:

One Man's Tribute To A Woman He Cannot Forget.

1.   Glover, Robert   2. Self-Help, Inspirational.

2.   Grief Education.

ISBN-13:   978-1523286966

ISBN-10:   1523286962

Introduction

A beautiful, warm, caring, intelligent woman died not long ago. And she shouldn't have. Terminal disease and death however, are two things we have no control over, but knowing this does absolutely nothing for me.

In his brilliant play "BECKET", author Jean Anouilh wrote that "death visits us all, even Archbishops." A lifelong faithful Catholic, I always admired Thomas Becket. He didn't seek martyrdom, but did not run from it, either.

So it was - and still is - with my feelings for Geraldine Lee Fish: I fell in love with her instantly, and for 21 years, carried that proverbial torch unashamedly. Yet, as she fought to live for three years, I was unaware of her plight.

When she approached the end of her life, however, I was excluded from it. Not by Gerri – she would never do that to me. When I decided to write this book, initial approval turned to cold silence and finally hostility.

A letter meant for me took eight months to arrive – after I learned she had passed. Only calling the Dayton Hospice succeeded in breaking through the wall of indifference erected by others.

I began writing these words on a quiet, chilly Thanksgiving Thursday in Newport, Kentucky. The sun was setting and I had walked clear to Covington and back. I met almost no one coming or going, and saw just a few people in or outside the Levee.

It was like being part of a small cast in one of those post-apocalypse, Sci-Fi tales. I've been a writer for 40 years, ever since my early college days at U. of D.

Sometimes I needed a day job, or I was able to work from home .There have been countless movies reviewed, meetings with Roger Ebert , Gene Siskel, and other, wonderful interviews and associations.

There was Pope John Paul II's first visit to Canada, and Queen Elizabeth's Royal Visit to Ontario, Canada, both in 1984. Her Royal Consort, Prince Philip, and I enjoyed some lively conversation while officials struggled for ten minutes to start their limousine.

There were my articles on the Edmund Fitzgerald tragedy as several important anniversaries of that Great Lakes tragedy were observed. Articles that had people calling me an 'expert' on the subject.

What do these events have to do with Gerry Fish, you might ask?

"Everything". This gift I am blessed with, you see, makes writing these pages the easiest thing I've ever done. I wanted to share my journalist's life with Gerry, not just episodes now and then, or just some of its perks - but everything.

Now I must live with only memories. There were the Club events, phone calls, the lovely Christmas cards, postcards

from her travels, and my visits to Dayton. She was the only reason for ever coming back, and the only person I wanted to share a very special, unforgettable Saturday with in 1987. There won't be any more new memories however, except those I make alone.

It has been that way for several years now, and I must accept this fact.

CONTENTS

The Minute I Saw The Three Typewriters, I Knew
This Was The Card For You". Given to Me by Gerry
For My 36th Birthday, April 28th, 1989

Special Thanks To Eileen Grauer, Campbell Co. ,Ky.
Your Warm Smile, Kind Heart, and Friendly Wave –
They All Did More Good Than You Know.

Bernard Malamud (1914-1986) for writing his
Pulitzer-Prize winning novel "The Fixer". Since that first read
in high school, I have ALWAYS owned a copy.

YOUR book helped me finish THIS book.

ACKNOWLEDGEMENTS

Gaynell Durham and Marva Busbee, Day Mont West Behavioral Health Care Dayton, Ohio. (Photos and Memories).

Gerald Wildenhaus, President, Catholic Alumni Club, Dayton, OH Chapter. Photos, Memories, Friendship.

Tom Rittenhouse, Administrative Assistant, Anderson H.S., Anderson, Ind. Senior Year High School Photo.

Gregory Wood, Dayton, Ohio. (Funeral Poem)

Debi "Duchess" Draper, Christopher Oaks, Rachel "Slugger" Mick ,"'Queen"' Elizabeth Van Dyke, Adult Reference; Natalie 'Road Kill ' Ruppert, Circulation Director,

Kenton Co. Public Library, Erlanger, Ky.

JANUARY 12TH, 1983: THE WONDERFUL NIGHT I DIED.

The Dayton, (OH). Catholic Alumni Club chapter no longer plays volleyball on Sundays at Bergamo Center. I regret very much hearing about this, and also how the club, once 200 members strong, has now shrunk to around 20 people.

I had attended several CAC functions in late 1982, but "the fishes" - Gerry and her sister Kathy - were with family in Ft. Wayne, Indiana. Then came that third Sunday, with Kathy and myself playing on the same team.

Gerry had business elsewhere, and wouldn't arrive until later. Now, 30 years later, as with everything else about her, the moment is still crystal clear. I saw Gerry over on the sidelines, mingling with club members.

She wore a light green jacket, white blouse, and orange pants.

At intermission, as the teams and players rotated, CAC member Sue Berger took me over to meet our club President. I looked into those green eyes, at that immaculate face, and those beautiful brown curls that I would eventually caress again, and again.

It was like being mildly electrocuted, in a pleasant way: I couldn't move, only shake her hand, introduce myself and stare, unable to let go. From somewhere far away, I seemed to hear an "ER" - type medical voice pronounce me dead on arrival. "If this is death", I thought, let it kill me again and again.

WATCH THE VOLLEYBALL, DUMMY, NOT HER.

Falling in love has its risks, and falling for Gerry Fish was flat out dangerous.

Our volleyball night resumed for its second half, and our teams rotated. Gerry moved around the gym, mixing with people as club president. First she was to my left, then directly behind our team, and then to my right. I followed her everywhere with my eyes.

Every few seconds, I turned back, while still contributing my personal best to the game. After yet another glance, I returned to the game, which was rapidly escalating. A minute or two of concentration was all I could spare, however, because once again my eyes traveled across the gym to find HER. Unfortunately, my body was facing the net, hands outstretched awaiting the serve. So it was that my eyes found Gerry just as the volleyball found me. Several girls helped me to my feet. MORAL: Playing volleyball means watch the game, not the DAME.

I'LL HAVE BEER, PIZZA, AND THAT FISH.

After volleyball the players always reconvened at Marion's Pizza, a few blocks away. This Sunday night was part of a long weekend for many, as the King Holiday was being observed the next day.

I made myself comfortable at a table with several of the guys, and we were joined by various ladies off and on. One of them was Gerry, and she would visit my table three times before the night was over.

Don't blame me: I didn't force her.

We covered all the bases without haste: occupation, schools, colleges, what brought me back into the CAC, etc.   Each visit lasted longer than the one before it, until finally I could stand the temptation no longer.

I HAD to ask her out; and as we say today, failure was not an option for me. I remember her reply to this day: "Well, I am sort of seeing someone right now, but I would still love to go out with you sometime," she said. And as I looked into those beautiful green eyes, and listened to that perfectly enunciated response, I realized there really is a God after all.

FEB. 17TH-18TH, 2012: A TRIP NO MAN SHOULD EVER HAVE TO TAKE.

Saturday is the last day of the week

Some people sleep in this morning, while others run errands, or maybe just "suit up" and run a few miles. For me, Saturday September 19th, 1987, was a day where I observed history being made - with an absolute beauty beside me.

Now, almost 25 years later, I sat in a Knight's Inn motel room, awaiting a phone call from Gerry's younger sister (by 14 months) Kathleen. CNN was covering the arrivals and preparations for Whitney Houston's funeral, but my feelings were committed elsewhere.

The decision - made several months before - was easy enough: travel to Dayton as our Metro Detroit school districts let out for February Break, and see where Gerry lies.

I checked in around 4 p.m., watched some of "31 Days of Oscar" on TCM, then walked around the Dayton Mall before visiting its food court. Was I retracing the same walk I'd made with her so long ago?

No; I prepared well for this time, even getting some counseling the previous week. I kept a scheduled appointment with a non-denominational Minister, prior to leaving for Dayton, we both agreed, "as a precaution."

Breakfast Saturday morning was at my favorite place - the Waffle House - then I went back to the motel until Kathy arrived. The "catching up" as we drove to Calvary Cemetery can be skipped.

I did not travel 200 miles four years after my own mother's passing to recount small talk. As we entered the grounds everything was fine, with none of the nervousness I had expected.

We reached the family's plot, and walked over to a trio of graves. Gerry is on the far right, after her father and grandmother. Behind us were the plots already chosen for Kathy, Tom, and their two children. In late September, 2015, Gerry's mother passed away and now rests beside her.

Incredibly enough, I was still myself - but only for another moment. As I began recalling that wonderful January night, in the time it takes to speak a single word, my heart shattered all over again. The memory of our first meeting at Bergamo was too much. At least today I only "tear up" whenever I think about it.- like now.

How many times have I returned to that first night since hearing the awful news, since finally getting her last letter? Pointless as it certainly Is, how many times have I wished I could have looked into the future that night and seen her destiny? And having seen it, done – what?

We can't change the past, or the future, because even that is probably a done deal. I poured my heart out that afternoon: hating what had happened to her, describing the pain I was feeling and the tremendous love I still felt for her. Not caring who knew it.

Not everyone, perhaps, will like what I am doing, and as such they should remember a very important fact. She's dead; and realizing that, ask yourself what harm can this tribute do?

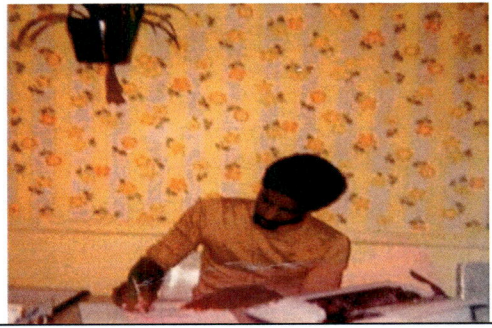

Once Upon A Time, We Did Use
Pens, Paper, and Portable Typewriters.

THE FIRST DATE (BUT NOT THE LAST).

Two weeks is not a long time, generally speaking. When you fall for someone however – and fall HARD - it can be a lifetime. I finally had something to suggest for a perfect outing:

A Tahitian Dance company was appearing at Memorial Hall in Dayton, and I asked Gerry to take in a Sunday matinee with me.

An article I wrote for my Detroit paper, promoting in advance the troupe's visit there got me free tickets for it locally. As talented as the dancers were, as tasty in their tropical attire, I had someone much more interesting beside me.

Not even the thick, long black hair flowing down their backs had the same effect on me as my beautiful, brunette companion. I watched Gerry almost as much as I did the performers, wanting to take her hand in mine, but dreading the consequences of it.

Even now writing these lines is difficult, and I know without a second thought that breaking off here is certainly best for me.

The Dayton Mall has changed a lot since then, as I saw last February. Yet I still remember how it was on that so perfect Sunday evening. We did not rush, and no business other than Gerry's stopping to pick up a gift for someone.

We walked around slowly, reviewing the matinee just attended, and getting to know each other better. We sat down for a while beside a large, circular water fountain, continuing to talk.

There were my years at U. of D., and her work with the Red Cross after she graduated from Wright State. Looking at you, Gerry, was like being pinned to the spot by an unseen force.

I could talk, think, even notice people walking by, but they did so in slow motion without making a sound. Deciding to eat, we also elected not to visit one of the restaurants.

"Too noisy; I want us to be able to hear each other," you said. So we settled on the Food Court, although I don't remember now what either of us ordered.

Five years apart in age, and yet so many little things in common.

She attended St. Helen's Catholic Church, while - until our family left WPAFB - I worshiped at the Base chapel half a mile away. We lived in "off-base" military housing; Gerry and Kathy were just two miles away in Georgetown Apartments.

So near, and yet, as they say, so far. Always like two trains leaving the station on parallel tracks –but just minutes apart. Consequently, one never sees the other - until fate brings them together on a Sunday night.

Had there not been a recession I would have remained in Dayton. I would have tried to cultivate the budding romance and overpowering feelings that were so obvious.

Gerry came along when my parents were divorcing after many years. Our mother moved back to Detroit, my stepfather remained at the base, and I moved into the Dayton YMCA.

Work was not plentiful, my Volkswagen very unsympathetic, and only selling off my classic movie soundtracks kept me in room rent. Yet I received a blessing on that January night, and now she lies beneath a headstone.

I always wanted to get that next journalism break in Columbus, Greenville, Xenia, anywhere close enough for me to "court" her again. When the chance finally came, little did I know that uterine cancer would be my rival.

I called her one more time after what became our last meeting: "I've been off work for a while because something's wrong with my stomach", she said. Her last words to me were, "I am seeing my doctor; "don't worry, Robert, it is probably nothing".

Only that last letter, mass-mailed after she died, explained what followed There are times however, when even looking at it on my wall is not enough, and the healing I have accomplished vanishes in an instant.

Now I am finally living here again - just an hour from where we first met. I have come back, but the one thing I always cherished most is gone. Now I must be content to talk to a ghost. A ghost who, while living, survived one cancer - only to be killed by another. And YES, I am angry. Because, I want HIM to tell me "WHY"?

DRIVING ROBERT HOME: A.K.A. "THE SET-UP."

Two weeks later it happened that we carpooled to Volleyball together. How is it that, even in the jeans and sweatshirt you changed into, your beauty was still enough to blind a man? And, like the month before, another "Fish" was on my team, YOU.

I don't remember much about that night, except that you weren't wearing any makeup. Not that this mattered; you still turned men's heads all across the gym. Then came our stopover at Marion's Pizza, and after a while, it was time for us to leave.

"I'm taking Robert home, and then I have to drop off some flyers to a couple of people," you said. Well, some of that was true. As we sat in your car, warming it up, all I could do was look.

That electric current I had felt upon our first meeting was back, while my stomach churned like cake batter in a mixing bowl. The impulse to kiss you was unbearable, but I restrained myself.

How could I know that chivalry was about to meet its match?

We reached their apartment and Gerry made me comfortable, showing me around while remarking that we could drop the flyers off later. "Both members live on the way to your place," she said, gently.

My memories of the apartment are that it was large, and the living room very spacious. Its decorations are now vague memories, but the moment that Gerry so deftly engineered is not.

She had taken a phone call and was walking around in small circles, twirling the cord and drawing closer to where I stood. The call ended, and standing flush up against me, Gerry put down the phone. Her eyes told the whole story: "don't just stand there, do something".

An unseen voice urged me to "get her, get her now. Kissing Gerry was the easiest thing I'd ever done with any woman; She just slid right into my arms, her mouth opening like a delicious bear trap.

We slammed against the wall as one, without disturbing even one object. My hands went everywhere - and Gerry's were just as busy. When you're in love with a woman, as I already was with her, sometimes polite restraint belongs someplace else.

There was no talking, just lots of furious foreplay, until we jointly came up for air. And, when Kathy arrived, there was no mad scramble to conceal our mutual misbehavior. We had remained fully clothed, not even draping our bodies across the sofa, and everything looked right as rain.

There was some surprise at my being there, but Gerry simply explained she had invited me to visit. I wonder, especially now, what went through her sibling's mind, and how often did she ponder on it?.

In time we left, and as Gerry allowed her car to briefly warm up, I raised the thermostat another way. I held her as hard as my arms allowed, squeezing her until I thought she would break.

No muffled protest came from her mouth, however, and when our lips parted, it was time to move off of each other, and move on. The flyers got delivered alright, and I got home - eventually.

Taking the long way around the barn sometimes is a lot of fun.

ST. PATRICK'S DAY, 1983: WHEN THE KITCHEN IS HOT, GRAB YOURSELF A FISH

Our CAC group held a St. Patrick's Day party that weekend .I believe it was in the clubhouse at Georgetown Apartments. By then, as if it needed explanation, I was totally gone on Gerry.

It is one thing to be so smitten with a woman, but in Gerry's case, just watching her navigate a crowded room was heavenly hell. Knowing that she was watching you, seeing those green eyes locked on me after mine had already sought her out, was the sweetest torture imaginable.

Even now I don't need this old photo to remember what she wore: a bright green skirt which ended just above the knees, and a silky white blouse with frills across its bosom. I took the picture just as she turned towards the camera.

She is slightly surprised at what I am doing. There's a Tostitos chip in her mouth. The photo's age makes me long to take it all over again. Unfortunately, her position as club President put her out of my reach for much of the evening. Fortunately, she had kitchen duty as well, along with several other women and guys.

Myself included. It was perfectly natural, therefore, to wait on people and keep the punch bowls filled. To make small talk with Gerry and wait. Wait for the perfect opportunity to be alone with her – and pounce.

Then at some point - when I don't exactly remember - my persistence and amorous designs suddenly paid off. The kitchen was staffed by just Gerry and another club member, who was busy at the window counter.

Gerry asked me to help her get more punch - or something - from the supply closet. I followed her around the corner, trying to ignore those fantastic legs before me and the back of her head with those gently bouncing, reddish brown curls.

I loved the way she walked; such perfect, lady-like poise, and the immaculate way she framed every word when she talked. The instant we were out of sight, I slipped my arms around Gerry's waist and pulled her to me.

I crushed my lips to hers, pushed us against the wall, and dug my fingers into her hair - hard. I could hear the voices of more girls in the kitchen, but the potential threat of discovery didn't discourage me.

I kissed Gerry long and hard until that pesky voice sounded again - urging me to cease fire immediately. I would describe the look on her face as our lips parted, and the feeling which occupied my lower regions -   Gerry gradually smoothed down her skirt and adjusted the perfectly fitting blouse as I picked up the supplies she had come for. We returned to the kitchen, making the most natural and innocent entrance. Fruit punch has never tasted better - before or since.

Thinking Of You On Good Friday, Mar. 25th, 2016.

I honestly don't know why I did not see this entry would be necessary. I originally wrote it for my Kindle version in 2013, while sitting on some pillows in my living room.

My fingers began guiding the pen I held across the paper before me. Then it was done. "We dated here (Dayton), and we dated there (Columbus)." "We even got together in Canada twice."

"Now I sit here alone - it is so unfair."

All those years, I pursued a career "break", and when it finally came, so did your undeserved fate. First the uterine cancer, then those damned adrenal gland tumors, the blocked bowel, a blood infection, and much later, Pneumonia.

You got sick, and then you got better, but it did not last. Now I know that visiting you in Dayton Hospice was not to be. Watching you unresponsive and dying would have been too much for me.

Two years after Kindle, I am preparing this permanent tribute to you. One that will survive long after I and others mentioned here are long dead. You will be in Hospice libraries and hopefully public ones, too.

Your face will shine forth from the AMAZON 'Books' home page. Ten days from now, surgery is scheduled to help me begin home dialysis, should it become necessary.

Time and time again, I return to how much you suffered, and your numerous medicine bottles – compared to my paltry six. It is thoughts like these that have sustained me through the rejection and resentment which reared their ugly head.

I could say I never loved you, deny my feelings for you, and be done with it. Unfortunately, as Mr. Malamud's title hero said in his novel, "the Fixer", "telling lies takes a talent I haven't got."

SUMMER, 1983: A NIGHT IN "CAMELOT", A NIGHT IN HEAVEN.

A RECESSION, AS WE ALL KNOW TOO WELL, DISRUPTS LIVES AND DASHES HOPES.

Winter ended in Dayton, Spring came, and I elected to try Columbus.

Another CAC member arranged for me to board with her sister and a friend in a suburb, Minerva Park. I found some work here and there, through KELLY and MANPOWER offices. I almost got my foot in the door at the city's other daily paper, The Citizen-JOURNAL.

One day I drove past a theatre whose name I've since forgotten.

Richard Harris would be appearing soon in a road tour of "Camelot". I had already interviewed him two years earlier in Detroit. My Detroit paper wanted our chat updated, and the Columbus theatre cleared me for the press conference.

Complimentary tickets? Yes; two.

Thus the stage was set to watch "King" Richard at work again. This time, however, with a piece of Heaven sitting beside me. Of course Gerry said 'yes' when I called her up about the tickets, and the date for Press Night.

I offered to pay for her gas if she wanted to drive to Columbus. What happened next was almost like the Fates had decreed it themselves. "I will be in Columbus for a two day Social Work conference," she said.

My heart exploded with joy, and we made plans to contact each other when she got to town. So, on a Wednesday July night, I pulled up to the front of her hotel and a sight which always left me breathless.

Gerry was standing there, perfectly poised as usual, smiling gently. The outfit she had chosen was stunning and unforgettable: peach-colored, its short, waist-length jacket barely concealed the matching blouse beneath it, or the outline of her breasts.

The skirt, although modest and very proper, did absolutely nothing to hide her fantastic legs, or control my blood pressure. I got out of the car and went around to open the passenger side door.

As she took her seat and smoothed down her skirt, I tried not to look again: forlorn hope. I don't remember everything we talked about - what Mr. Harris was like and his salty tongue mostly -was like and his "salty" tongue mostly – en route to the theatre and after we arrived in the lobby.

Every time I looked at you I risked going blind.

Whenever I did, every nerve in my body buzzed and shook with excitement. How many times did I glance at you and find myself unable to turn away? How many times did you turn to me so ever so slightly with that gentle smile on your face?

I pause every few strokes while writing this part. I do so because, while remembering is easy, what we remember best is what makes us suffer the most. During the After Glow hour – how appropriate a name for that night I introduced you to Richard Harris, watching later as you chatted with him across the room and he drowned in your beauty.

We both know he did; who wouldn't have?

How is "King Richard" doing today? Have you two met again by now? I could not see the many interviews that still lay ahead for me -

Sandy Dennis, Patty Duke, Anthony Hopkins, William Windom, and one very special Papal Visit.

I could only see you as we walked back to my car and sat on the front seat for several minutes. I suggested going someplace else, but you replied softly, "its late". When I leaned over and kissed you on the cheek, you responded with a hug - and I found myself unable to let go.

I can still smell that perfume; , the softness of you is still fresh 30 years later, and I hear the rustle of that lovely outfit as my hands caress your body. And suddenly, there was no escaping the kiss that I was determined to deliver.

How long we locked together on that front seat I don't know, but it was the closest thing to Paradise this man has ever experienced. My hands went everywhere - as did yours - and I made a complete mess of your fabulous hairdo.

Eventually you did find Paradise – but left me behind in the process. And there's not a damned thing I can do about it now.

Thanks to You, I Had The Time of My Life.

PEOPLE SAY "MEN DON'T LEAVE": THAT'S A LIE - BECAUSE MEN DO.

Writing this part is especially hard for me, and not because several other men are in it. Yes, I still feel some jealousy because they were a part of your life, but also a little anger.

Why, some may ask? Because they all left you.

I don't pretend to know the reasons, and I am not judging anyone. But let's face it fellas: I am very biased – and don't like the way you treated this particular lady. Are you the reasons she is no longer here? Did He take Gerry to spare this beautiful woman from being alone too much more?

Did He ever consider my feelings for Gerry, and that I might want to spend the rest of my life with her? Sorry guys, no names have been changed, so read on.

THE ONE WHO WENT SOUTH.

Remember that night, Gerry? I called you up and we talked about many things; eventually I asked, As always, if you were seeing anyone, testing the romantic waters once again. You told me about this Army guy, his liason job the base, and then his transfer to Florida. After he left, SILENCE.

"I guess I had a different view of the relationship than he did," you said. I just listened; letting Gerry unburden her soul, while hurting in my own way for her. "Its really too bad, Robert," you said, "because we were really hot and heavy for a while."

It was the dead of Winter, but your fires had gone out..

Picturing you sitting there alone in that large, 2- bedroom Georgetown apartment, hurting, was no fun, Princess. Not then, and not now. Now I know all the facts. So, 'General", you were seeing other girls in the club behind my Gerry's back.?

Or so I heard. Do you know that she's gone? Are you still out there somewhere? Do you even care? Congratulations on being made a GS-12 too, my man. Too bad character and compassion were not included .I'll bet Florida was nice in Winter time.

WITH NORM YOU ALMOST TIED THE KNOT.

Now married and moved on, I located Norm living out of state,

but he declined to participate in this enterprise. Our current CAC Dayton chapter president tells me that he and Gerry were "close to an engagement at one point, but it never happened".

So tell me Norm, what went wrong? I never intruded on Gerry's personal life or romances. - After all, I was four hours away, and long distance is long distance. He said you came to visit her in Hospice just before she died, and I type these lines knowing I could never have done that - it would have killed me.

When we talked briefly, you said "our relationship was very special, and she was very special to a lot of people." You didn't seem too pleased when I said "Gerry was very special to me, too". Did I hit a sour note, or two?

I think about her every day, Norman; I just want you to know that. When you read these lines, you will see that I did finish this book, for Gerry's sake and her memory, whether some people like it or not.

She deserves this tribute, not just because I loved her so much, but because people need to know about her. Maybe after I visit her Easter Week, some of the pain will go away. Maybe.

NOTE; On October 6th, 2013, as I prepared to email the first copies of the Kindle version of this work, word came that Norm passed away in Louisville, KY., Oct. 2.

Perhaps one day we can all sit down and talk things over.

I HEAR YOU'RE MARRIED TOO – JUST NOT TO MY PRINCESS.

One year ago this coming Saturday, Kathy and I were driving back from Calvary Cemetery and I asked about other men in her life. When she got sick, that is. Your name came up – "Jay" isn't it? – And Kathy said "they were together a long time, then they broke up, and I was hoping they'd get back together but they never did."

So you're the reason why two of my visits weren't as pleasant as so many, many, others. I can understand Gerry getting involved with someone else – I had no claim on her – only my tremendous love.

Yet once again, she ended up alone, and once again I wonder what happened? What always went wrong? What was so difficult about making d keeping this lovely woman happy?

I know I could have –but God and two cancers chose not to give me that chance, and it HURTS. Did you visit her in Hospice, Jay, or had you married and moved on? Maybe that wouldn't have looked right; visiting dying, former girlfriend. Either when she was responsive, or later when she was comatose.

I always wanted happiness for Gerry – with someone else if not me – but that afternoon I faced the heart wrenching truth: she had died "alone" – without someone special in her life.

Cynthia (Bruger) Rose, who will speak later, said "I was always hoping she would get married, but I guess that just wasn't in the cards." What WAS in those cards, including the cruelty of Gerry spending her last months in a wheelchair or on a walker is devastating for me.

How devastating, you ask? Well, it is a wonder I can still write these words. Are Jerry W. and I the only men who still remember her? Do these others just shrug her off with a "well, that   was too bad about Gerry Fish"? If so, when God passed out hearts, he miscounted by at least three.

THE LONELINESS OF THE LONG-DISTANCE LOVER

Recessions can wreak havoc on a populace: people lose jobs, families lose their homes,

pets are left behind in garages with food, water, and pick up notes. The recession of the early 1980's took me from Detroit, Michigan back to Dayton, Ohio, then on the road looking for work.

Three months later, I am back in Dayton, closing up our family's quarters at WPAFB as my parents' divorce and my mother moves to Michigan. I check into the YMCA, work at K-Mart on Salem Avenue, and collect unemployment checks from "home".

Our "Camelot" night in Columbus was the brightest of any that I spent with you, Gerry, before fate, bad luck and a wrong decision pulled us apart.

Even now I procrastinated writing this section, because both knowledge – and the unknown that contains is too painful. In one instant, two stolen unemployment checks saw me evicted from the Columbus flat I shared and headed home to Detroit, Michigan.

I was tired, and discouraged, but still wanting to return to Ohio – and of course, my close proximity and budding relationship with Gerry. I eventually landed a job in a suburban school district – but one that put me out of state – and you out of immediate reach.

I hate this moment of indecision and cursed luck even more now that you are gone. Hate it because what we eventually had is not what I wanted. Long distance is long distance; 210 miles worth. It affected this relationship, changed how often two people talk, how often they saw each other.

How far would we have gone had I returned to Columbus? Certainly I would have seen you more often – maybe to where we got "serious" or embarked on a long-term relationship. – Perhaps there would have been a break-up, like with those other guys. Maybe we would have reconciled once, twice, thrice, or perhaps for good.

Or never.

It's what we did have for so long versus what we never had which haunts me now – and of course, there's no way of knowing what might have been – only where you are today. As I write these lines, you have been gone another year this month.

I decided to visit Dayton – and you – only after the Amazon copies arrive, but just the thought of them in my hands creates nervous excitement. Will there ever be an "anniversary" that becomes my last outpouring of grief? Probably not.

I say "last" because although the spells continue to come, the really bad ones are fewer and farther between. Three good things came of our family's assignment to WPAFB: my attending and graduation from U. of D., accidentally becoming a writer, and meeting you. Unfortunately, one is no good without the other.

Yet I go on, because there is too much more I want to write about. During my years as a writer, movie special effects have gone from being hand and camera-made to CGI. Newspapers and magazines are going digital – or just going away.

Twice I have felt your presence around me – the first a week after leaving the hospital (see page 66). What perfume did you fill my bedroom with that evening? I have to believe, whenever these moments of real grief come, that I will see you again one day. My counseling Pastor in Hazel Park, Michigan told me I will.

Hopefully this is not too much to ask.

When my time on this earth does end I pray it will be you who comes for me. Your mother said "we all miss her a lot." Hearing about you after the fact or not, I miss you a lot, too. I have cried much since hearing about you, Princess. And I wonder how much more crying there is for me to do.

I wonder if I will ever share my life with anyone else – like I wanted to with you. Nothing I accomplished up in Michigan – the public access A & E show for five years, covering John Paul II's Toronto stopover, the interviews with Sandy Dennis, James MacArthur, etc., ever made me feel really complete.

To enjoy that feeling meant having you, and I didn't.

Even the two newspaper jobs I eventually landed were in the wrong part of Ohio – North not South – and far from Dayton, Ohio. You have become the yardstick by which everything I did is measured.

As I write these pages, looking forward to their completion, I also catalog my Regrets. I try to pretend that loving you for decades did not happen. I hurt over being shut out of the end of your life, not knowing why, and now being treated like a third –class passenger in 'steerage.'

Any man who doesn't cry over all the times he spent with you is a fool. Any man who didn't appreciate you, or stay with you, should confess that failure to God. Because in my eyes, Princess, they have sinned.

Jerry told me that some of the guys in the club found you "irritating"; "they said she could never seem to make up her mind, that she was too indecisive and it really got on their nerves," said Jerry.

I wish you were here now – and you could be as indecisive as all get out. I would welcome it; you could irritate me until the cows come home, and I would love every second of it.

Instead you are somewhere else – in a place I cannot go. Not yet.

STARS EVERYWHERE - ANN ARBOR, 1985,'86.

The Ann Arbor Summer Festival was fun while it lasted.

A month long celebration of the performing arts, this venue brought in actors, actresses, playwrights, singers, dance companies, etc. Writers like myself had a ball covering it, and racking up some of my best interviews.

Truth be told however, no one - not Marcel Marceau, nor Kevin McCarthy, William Windom, even Clair Bloom in all her loveliness - could match the brightness given off by this woman who accepted my invitation.

What was the model of that car you drove for so long? All I remember now is its dark blue color, and how I would stare at you sitting behind the wheel

We were both worried about it not being up to the trip, but that June weekend we met in Ann Arbor. You had missed the Festival Preview and "Afterglow" - along with a chance to meet William Windom, my first scheduled interview - but no worry.

I checked you into the Motel 6 where I was staying, and we went into downtown to walkabout and eat dinner. Once again I was in the presence of great poise and beauty; once more the feeling of electric current ran through me.

My heart pounded non-stop, and I fought the urge to stare at you without collapsing into a trance. You appreciated the humor of James Thurber and Windom's one-man presentation; several times you touched me gently while laughing, and it was the greatest feeling in the world.

We sat on a restaurant terrace later, in a corner, enjoying the night air and a couple of drinks. The inevitable moment came when I embraced you and we kissed - in full view of other customers.

Separating, you smiled at me and said, "that's all for right now, get me back to the motel." Looking back on that evening, I like the way it ended: watching you go to your room and then turning to enter mine.

There was still another venue awaiting us, and more memories. Mr. Windom passed away in 2012: does he entertain you now with his wit, or has he told you about our terrific interview. Have you met Marcel Marceau again?

Remember Kevin McCarthy as President Truman in "Give Em' Hell Harry - any sign of him there? I remember our phone call when you returned to Dayton that first summer, and how your voice glowed with contentment.

"I had such a wonderful time, Robert; when can we do something like that again?" The answer would come the next year, with another Summer Festival.

Until then, I adored you in my mind, my love waiting.

SEPT. 18TH AND 19TH, 1987: POPE JOHN PAUL II DOES DETROIT AND A BEAUTIFUL FISH HELPS OUT.

OUR SCHEDULE WITH HIS HOLINESS

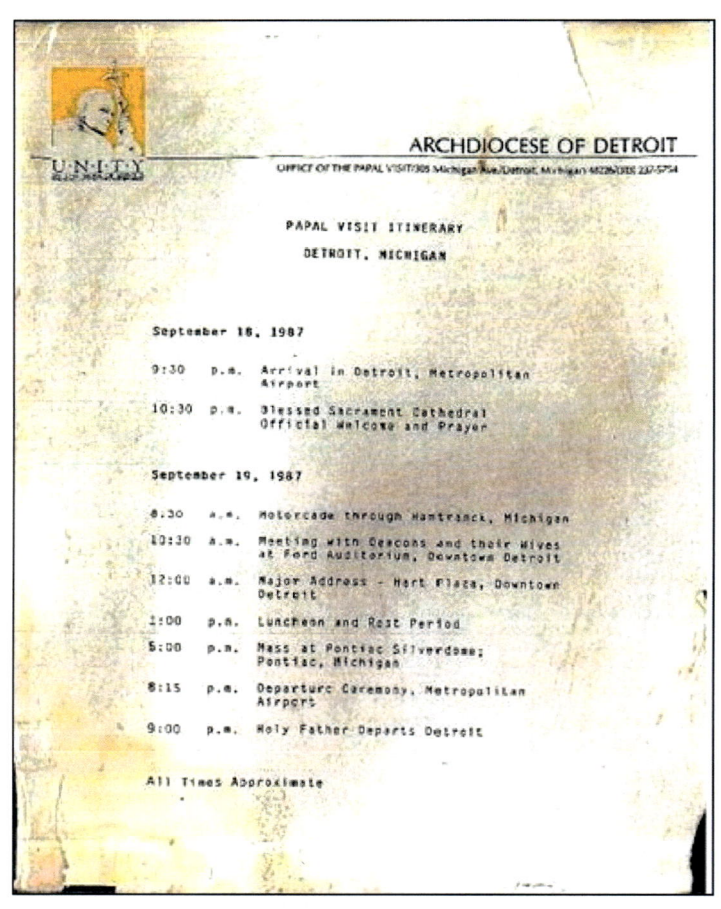

ARCHDIOCESE OF DETROIT

OFFICE OF THE PAPAL VISIT/305 Michigan Ave./Detroit, Michigan 48226/305 237-5754

PAPAL VISIT ITINERARY

DETROIT, MICHIGAN

September 18, 1987

9:30	p.m.	Arrival in Detroit, Metropolitan Airport
10:30	p.m.	Blessed Sacrament Cathedral Official Welcome and Prayer

September 19, 1987

8:30	a.m.	Motorcade through Hamtramck, Michigan
10:30	a.m.	Meeting with Deacons and their Wives at Ford Auditorium, Downtown Detroit
12:00	a.m.	Major Address - Hart Plaza, Downtown Detroit
1:00	p.m.	Luncheon and Rest Period
5:00	p.m.	Mass at Pontiac Silverdome; Pontiac, Michigan
8:15	p.m.	Departure Ceremony, Metropolitan Airport
9:00	p.m.	Holy Father Departs Detroit

All Times Approximate

ACT I: SHE MAKES HER ENTRANCE.

Today the South Bound side of 9 Mile and John R in Hazel Park sports a Tim Horton's and a CVS Pharmacy. 25 years ago, it was the site of a Holiday Inn, and without question the meeting of all meetings.

On Friday night, Sept. 18th, 1987, I waited inside its main lounge, watching the outside hallway through a glass window. The sight I awaited was one whose beauty rivaled even the Creation.

Her reason for coming to me had begun with a simple phone call to Dayton weeks before. My newspaper had been granted two guest passes for Pope John Paul 11's Detroit stopover.

I had also covered His Toronto visit in 1984 - but Detroit was a last-minute addition to his schedule, first announced in January. "Would you like to come up here and be a part of the Press pool,?" was my question. Gerry's answer was the same one that I never tired of hearing – as was and the gentle teasing in her voice.

"Are you sure you don't want to invite anyone else?," she asked. No beautiful; I didn't want to invite anyone else: not even super-cute Ann Monnin, or that wonderful nurse Karen (can't remember last name).

You were always the one; for this very special time and all the others .I took down your information and submitted it to the Archdiocese. They passed it on to the Secret Service, who ran a background check on you.

That night when you arrived, I saw the happiness and excitement on your face. We were about to embark upon a "pilgrimage" - one might say - and now both you and the man who brought us together are gone.

I still remember what you wore that night: a turquoise jacket, green pants, and white blouse. We watched the Pope disembark His plane at Metro Airport and head for Detroit, my stomach churning wildly.

If there is one regret, it is that I had to share you with someone else. Sure, your car couldn't make the trip - you said as much weeks before. When I offered to get you a room at the Holiday Inn, as God is our witness, you asked me THAT question again: "are you talking about sharing a room?"

I suggested that we see if one of your girlfriends from CAC would be Making the trip before committing to this; gossip and innuendo back home you did not need.

In the end, I behaved myself totally, until we walked around the hotel parking lot. On that warm September night, History waiting in the wings, I turned into an octopus.

BUT THAT IS ANOTHER STORY.

ACT TWO: SEPT. 19TH, 1987: THE DAY WE MADE HISTORY - TOGETHER.

You and Norm arrived at my house early that Saturday morning. It was overcast and temperatures were mild, as we headed downtown to Hart Plaza, where His Holiness was due to speak after visiting Hamtramack.

The front seats are where I still wish we both had been - but I was the Guest - and fate had put us in separate states several years before. Now, we were together for just a day, instead of a whole weekend.

Thanks to the Guest Pass, you were mine and Norm had to fend for himself while you fended me off every now and then. I watched you make your way around the Plaza, talking to people and getting their impressions of His visit.

I had wanted to include you in this adventure, this accomplishment. And the joy I experienced watching you is still indescribable.

ACT THREE: THE VIEW FROM ABOVE, THE VIEW FROM BELOW, AND YOU.

From downtown Detroit and the Plaza, it's a short, twenty minute drive North to the Pontiac Silverdome. It was here that His Holiness would celebrate the main High Mass of his stopover.

We traveled to our destination as the sun constantly tried to decide whether to show its face or allow gloom to rule the day. Upon arriving, for a few minutes, we were a trio once again. As I reflect on that interlude, I realize only one of us now remains - and wonder why.

I also reflect on something which should surprise no one by now. Why, for God's sake, were you so damned beautiful no matter what you wore? I can still see that dark, Navy Blue suit after all these years: the pockets with their large buttons, the matching skirt that failed miserably at hiding those bombshell legs.

You may have considered yourself dressing "conservatively", but let's face facts, Princess: you were a show-stopper. And there were those tinted sun glasses that hid your eyes so completely, yet I knew when you were looking at me so intently, and could read your thoughts with zero effort.

EPILOG: A LONG, DARK TUNNEL HAS ITS USES.

All things must pass, however, and so did our time as a trio. Norm went his way with the masses, and us together. No longer were you a Mental Health worker, from Daymont West but a member of — THE PRESS.

We joined that exclusive club - the press "pool" - and entered the tunnel off the Silverdome's main parking lot. The line was long, and people were pushed against each other over and over.

Suddenly you bumped against me, apologized with an "excuse me", and I pounced. Your body gave off an electric shock that was palpable, and I kissed those small, perfect lips with all my heart. The line had stalled for some reason, and I pushed you back against the wall behind us. I tried to crush the life out of you, Gerry, if only briefly.

Your arms felt so good around me, as did the caress of your lovely fingers. Unfortunately I had to release your mouth and guide us back into line - just as it resumed moving again. Just like the night before, I did not care who you were dating, or how serious it was, only that you had accepted my invitation and were standing next to me.

Now, waiting for us and everyone else at the end of this tunnel, was another moment not likely to be experienced by many people again. We wandered around the Press areas near the Altar, closer to Him than even people with paid admissions. You went this way and that - just like at Hart Plaza - glancing at me whenever I came into view again.

Now comes the part I must never forget: we were up in the stands again, and you were several rows in front of me. Close enough for me to see that radiant smile on your face when our eyes met.

I knew then just how happy I had made you. I must ALWAYS remember this. Because if I do not, there remains only the pain of knowing now what I did not know then: that you were doomed, and how much suffering would visit you, again and again.

DEC. 24TH, DEC. 25TH, 2012.. (FROM THE KINDLE EDITION).

"TIME IS A GENTLEMAN".

Leaving the Florence Mall on Christmas Eve, just before 5 p.m. The day was cloudy, cold, and full of reflection for me again. I hate Gerry being where she is - even though I know she is not really there.

This time of year is especially bad for me, because Gerry's final letter describes those last two holidays of her life. I try not to think about what she was feeling - and fail. Did she know this would be her last Thanksgiving and Christmas? Probably ot.

Was she prepared for the devastating news which awaited her in Texas afterwards? Certainly not. I think about these things and I cry, over, over, and over.

A year ago in Hazel Park I went to 11:00 a.m. Mass Christmas Morning - and was tearful the whole way through. This morning at Holy Spirit was different - there were no tears and my heart was not as heavy. No, I am not cured. Just still grieving, but on another level now.

NEW YEAR'S DAY, 2013

I sent a "Holiday Splendor" flower assortment to Cavalry Cemetery yesterday - bad weather two weeks running has delayed my visiting in person. I will go when it gets better, visit U. of D., buy a sweatshirt, etc. When I read the Oakwood Florist girl my book's title for the message card, she said, "very nicely put".

These simple words told me once again that what I have chosen to do with this book, is RIGHT.

AND WHEN SHE THOUGHT SHE WAS OUT OF THE WOODS - SHE WASN'T.

I have talked to Jerry Wildenhaus in January, February, and last night, Easter Sunday of all times. In two days we are to meet, and I feel like I've made a new friend - certainly someone who has been very helpful.

Also, I really believe, someone who misses Gerry as much as I do. He says "I was very fond of her", but I think he plays down his true feelings.

I think in our own ways, we both loved - and still love - her very much. What I learned this night made me sad – but determined to continue on.

"When Gerry thought she was out of the woods I got a call from her," said Jerry. "It seems she had scored a pair of tickets for a cruise for Cancer survivors along the Ohio River," he recalls.

I listened intently, and asked him "Can you remember what she wore? " "A button-down blouse - I don't remember the color, possibly a sort of red plaid, slacks, and a scarf - because she had lost her hair due to the chemotherapy - said Jerry.

"We took a picture together - someone else shot it for us - but now I don't know where it is," he said. A picture of them lost or mislaid; its final fate unknown, and our friend's own fate so unfair.

I knew while writing this that, come Easter Week, more of my questions would be answered. Until then the pain would continue. Jerry talked about how Gerry's family stored her "things" in a garage - "better than having a rummage sale, I think, to benefit strangers." he said.

I asked him if anybody had seen the multi-colored drinking cup - with Queen Elizabeth's likeness on it? Ontario had issued a limited number of them to mark Her Majesty's visit to Canada in October, 1984.

I had attended her Windsor stopover and "walkabout". I gave it to Gerry the Winter of 1987-88 (see next chapter). It is a late Christmas present", I had told her.

I knew by the way she studied me however, that Gerry wasn't buying it , Did she know what I was really saying? I think so, and if we believe in a Heaven, then I must also believe that now she knows for sure.

What is it like to pack up someone's life and simply put it away? Except for the times I have moved, the answer escapes me. Everything that was you, Princess, is now boxed up in Dayton. The image of you lives on in my mind, adorns my living room wall, or decorates my day planner cover.

It is not enough - Gerry; not by half. If I had only known about your situation, maybe I wouldn't be writing this today. Maybe I would be "over" you and moved on. Or maybe just died from the terrible grief I've experienced.

Jerry said that you "kept it very low-key". "OK, but by doing that, she denied me "closure' down the road," I said. Every morning that I awake, open my eyes and live another day I move on - but without 'closure'.

My church deacon said in January that "the consequence of having loved Gerry so much is the pain you are feeling now." He asked me to trust that God did what was best.

Believing this is very, very, hard.

October, 1986: Miss Sandy Dennis
Friendly, Funny, Lively, Informative
One of My Best Interviews, Ever.

Sandy died of ovarian cancer in April, 1992; she was just 54.

FEBRUARY, 1988: SNOW, SHIPS, SKATES, AND YOU.

Everything that followed in the wake of John Paul II's visit, paled by comparison as they say.

Everything except meeting screenwriter John Briley, along with (then) exiled white newspaper editor Donald Woods . Briley, whose screenplay for "Gandhi" had won him an Oscar, was promoting Richard Attenborough's anti-apartheid film "Cry Freedom", for which he had also written the screenplay.

The Winter Olympics were underway in Calgary, Alberta when I touched base with Gerry and learned she was coming to Windsor for her NOW (National Organization For Women) convention.

It was easy to ask her if we could get together - and no surprise that she said "yes". Remembering what followed makes me hesitate to type these lines, because simple pleasures are always the most beautiful.

Pleasures like seeing you walk into the Holiday Inn Windsor's lounge, smiling as we approached each other. till feel the warmth of your body as I released you, knowing that public affection made you nervous.

There was a lull in the convention activities - its main speaker not scheduled to speak until 10 o'clock or so - and we had two hours together. I chose a pair of sofas near the lounge's main window, which looked out onto the Detroit River.

Snow was falling steadily, and we both marveled at the closeness of the freighters that kept passing slowly by.

Christy Yamaguchi was America's favorite in the figure skating finals, and Gerry my favorite object to just watch. That's not true. I slipped my arms around her quietly, content just to hold this treasure and look into her eyes.

When we kissed it was so easy; natural and right. I tightened my embrace after she whispered "Robert, I won't break." Christy Y. stumbled badly twice, and we both knew she was finished. We enjoyed a couple of drinks, and watched snow falling on the river. More freighters passing by close enough to touch.

Our time together passed much too quickly, and suddenly Gerry had to go. We walked over to the auditorium, hugged again, and then she was gone.

OCTOBER 8TH, 1988: "THIS IS YOUR LIFE, GERRY FISH". (HER 40TH)

This flashback concerns more than just Gerry's milestone birthday. It is about a breakfast date and an afternoon in Carillon Park that I want back more than life itself. Of course, that's not possible - ever. one by one I had marked the days of September off, always looking ahead to October 8th, Gerry's 40th birthday.

I knew that her family would be throwing something huge for her, and that I couldn't spend the big date itself with her. Columbus Day, however, means a Monday holiday, and I put in for a personal business day from my Catholic school in advance.

I told Gerry as much, and also arranged to have dinner on her birthday with my best friend from U. of D. I walked around the Oregon District that Sunday, and passed the evening without doing anything special.

"Special" was the operative word for Monday morning, and breakfast at a Bob Evans Restaurant. Gerry picked me up at the motel, giving new meaning to the words, "casually dressed."

Did you really think, Princess, that blue jeans, a pullover sweater and jacket could hide that splendid, petite figure of yours? All I could do was smile and stare. If lightning had struck me down, I'd have felt nothing.

It was always this way with you, Gerry Fish.

We let the waitress seat us at a corner booth, and I listened to your descriptions of the 'surprise' birthday party. I still remember what was obviously its highlight - the montage your family had prepared entitled "This is your Life, Gerry Fish" - and your incredible smile.

I also remember being totally helpless as you ordered breakfast. Maybe it was the way you tilted your head ever so slightly, this way or that, Or was it those magnificent reddish- brown curls, the small, graceful fingers, or that soft, gentle, voice which held me prisoner?

Maybe it was the way you perfectly pronounced every word that seem to redefine anew the term "lady". I don't remember what we talked about that morning, but I still recall what is now, in my mind, the MOMENT.

We were ready to leave and you offered to split the tab with me - but I refused. Then you offered to get the tip - and I did likewise again. The look on your face - and the question you asked a week later on the phone said it all:

"I've been thinking a lot about when we were together Robert, the way you acted, how you treated me, the nice things you said -. "Robert", you asked, "are you in love with me?"

The answer I gave then is the same one I repeated at Calvary one year ago: "Yes", ever since the night I met you." And I still am. We left the Bob Evans, and drove to Carillon Park. There Gerry parked her car. There we listened to the bells, talking, touching, embracing. We left the car, walking around, holding hands and each other.

It was all so right, just like everything else that I remember: the color of your Wright State University ring the shape of your fingers, that lovely way you always said "oh really?" whenever I said something surprising.

I don't know if you were seeing anyone at that time and I wouldn't have cared anyway. The important thing is we were together. And for every time I touched you that day, there was always another visit where I dared not, because you were so damned beautiful.

Now, I can only touch a headstone, your picture, or that last letter you wrote over three months while in Hospice of Dayton. One thing is certain: I have loved you totally and purely, even if you did not always feel the same way about me.

There were never any arguments, no break-ups, or bad feelings between us. If there had been, would I be so forgiving and grieving now, or instead full of indifference and merely able to shrug your undeserved fate off?

Only two times did we meet and part on less than glowing terms. Considering that we knew each other for over twenty years, that is good.

Looking back on those two moments, I blame other things happening in your life at the time - and other people - for the lack of our usual affection.

But while looking back, I am glad that, despite this, we still parted friends. The affection would return soon enough. And who can say that mine has ever stopped?

HOLY WEEK 2013: A VISION REVISITED.

On Monday afternoon of Holy Week, royalty arrived in my mailbox. I knew what it was when I saw the envelope, and the address from Anderson, Indiana. I opened it once inside the apartment, and there you are in four different sizes.

It is your 1967 Senior class Yearbook photo. Everyone looks their best; you, Princess, look SUPERB. Perfect poise, lips together, smiling gently. Your hairdo reminded me instantly of Cindy Williams in "American Graffiti", with the front curved to one side.

BEAUTIFUL. Holy Wednesday, I placed it in my Yahoo! Inbox.

Now I had my first illustration for this book. I also had a copy of it laminated at FED EX Kinko's and now you sit beside me as I work. How many times have I looked at it at home, too, viewing your lovely visage with a heavy heart?

I also want to show you off to people as I work - let them see how lovely you were. How many more times will I look at it, and what will I feel when we are finally together again?

I missed so many wonderful times with you by living somewhere else: Sunday Mass together, "one-tank" car trips that I still love to take, the "perks" that came with my many story assignments.

Jerry said the CAC was "a big part of your life" -as I well know - and writing a huge part of mine. You were the perfect opposite for me, Gerry: your gentle way was needed to counter the tenacious side of my personality.

We never discussed those horrible times at U. of D., (see P. 100) or that one Saturday night there when I literally fought to stay alive. We never talked about race, and you didn't seem to mind my economic situation when we first met.

Now, looking at this splendid photo, I hurt when thinking of what lay ahead for you. I wonder who your first boyfriend was, and how many guys suffered like me just by looking at you.

It is Easter Monday now; on Good Friday I attended a CAC Fish Fry at St. Lawrence Church in Cincinnati. Do you remember Don Luebbering from all the CAC conventions, Princess?

He definitely remembers you; we sat and ate together, discussing my freelancing and work history. I told him I had a surprise with me, and I took out your Anderson, H.S. photocopies. "It doesn't even look like her", he said, but quickly realized the truth.

"A work in progress", was my reply, and he noted that you were "a real beauty both inside and out". Who can argue with that statement? We talked about my good times with you, but ultimately came to the real point.

"Why didn't tell me she'd been sick, or even later that she wasn't going to make it?" I asked him. Several times Don addressed the question, each time with a different answer. "Maybe she didn't want you to worry", he said, then later "she wasn't going to burden you with her illness," and, "she didn't want you to be hurt."

Fair enough, Gerry, but now perhaps, you see how hurt I still AM by not knowing. Maybe, just maybe, you dropped the ball here. Did you try to reach me or have someone else contact me? Did somebody take it upon themselves not to try because they did not know me that well?

No, I couldn't have endured Dayton Hospice, the service, or the burial and even now seeing a funeral procession pass by reopens the wounds. Jerry Wildenhaus gave me three photos of you at different club events, and some newsletters with your monthly message to everyone. Three years later, I still avoid reading them.

Top: Unknown, Marjie Knudson,
Fr. Jim Duell (Chaplain).
Front: Joan Myers,
Rick Bruns, Gerri.

I look at the Christmas Party photo from 1984, and wonder why you look so sad. Were you thinking of me, up in Michigan, where I had been pressured into remaining? The group pictures show off your stunning beauty, but break my heart at the same time.

You are gone from us forever, and I wonder if, to some of your friends, you are now just a memory.

TWO INTO ONE CAN GO

It is Easter Wednesday, and Jerry has left me at your grave to visit his people elsewhere in the cemetery. I feel very close to Jerry, like I've made a new friend. We have something in common, of course - YOU.

We met for lunch at Tim Horton's beforehand. Not at all like Norm the other night, which is why he became fair game in that previous entry. Hell; if they didn't know how to treat you and keep you, then they are all fair game to me.

Norm "wanted no part of it," (the book) and really talked down to me when reminding me "how special you were to a lot of people." In turn, I told him how special you were to me, too.

His voice noticeably dropped an octave as he replied, somewhat irritated, "yeah, I know." As Jerry said, "well excuse me for breathing". I wonder who else will react this way? I make no excuses Gerry: you deserve to be seen, and to be written about.

I came apart briefly when showing Jerry the flash drive - and two other times, but alone at Calvary in those moments - I was fine. I thought about that horrible disease, your tremendous suffering and how I miss you so much. Jerry says that when he visited you in Hospice once, the anger and bitterness was obvious. "I've been sitting here thinking, and feel I really don't deserve this," you said.

"It just so happens that I agree with you," said Jerry; "you got a raw deal." He remembered you noting he was the first person to say that, and I said the same when I first visited Calvary.

I need to know something, Princess: were you "okay" with it? Did you accept what God was doing to you? What was it like on that flight back from Houston? Did you cry, or just stare out the window, knowing how much time you had left and remembering your life?

Last year, as she drove me back to the Knight's Inn, Kathy said you went to Dayton Hospice, got your room ready, and set up the pain "meds".

Were they right, or did God decide to take you early?

These things trouble me, and they are the reason I MUST finish this book. If I don't, we will never know what could have been accomplished. All this will have been a waste of time, and the hurt will go on.

Maybe it is fortunate the freelance market is so bad right now. There is time for me to write. Jerry and I were at Tim Horton's about 90 minutes, and three times I broke down badly. Afterward , we drove up Wilmington Avenue to Dayton Hospice, by agreement.

Jerry took us across the grounds to that beautiful pond in back. The pond is really beautiful - but you already know that, don't you? He pointed to the window that had been your room, and told me how, when you could still sit in a wheelchair, you loved watching this scene.

I tried not to picture you in that room, at that window, or how "changed" you eventually looked. I don't want to think about how tired your body finally got, or when you could no longer get into the wheelchair - at all.

How Jerry could visit you I don't know - but maybe I am being too hard on myself. I spoke those very same words at your grave last year: my voice dry, my chest hurting terribly, and the tears coming on non-stop.

Yet your belief in "God's Grace" did not save you, and one of His miracles did not come. And I did not know your fate until much later. "We are all in prison, one way or another, and those who understand this suffer most of all. " - . Morris L. West, in his novel, "The Shoes of The Fisherman."

Gerry with Two Friends At A CAC Function; early 1990's.

THE END OF MY AFFAIR (ALMOST): SEPT. 19TH, 2011, 10:30 P.M.

This 'had to be included' recollection concerns my own close call with mortality. Not a near-miss from a crazy, cell-phone obsessed driver, or a run-in with some gang-banger wannabee or opportunist mugger.

I have met and survived all of them. Minus one front tooth.

Looking back, I should have checked "it" out: the gradually increasing tightness in my chest, feeling out of breath (and hurting after running for a SMART bus, or having to stop my morning, bare knuckle push-ups).

On Sept. 19th, 1987, we witnessed history together, and on this night 24 years later, I was thinking of you as my lungs failed me completely. The ambulance came quickly; I staggered out to meet it.

They put the oxygen mask over my face and we raced to St. John's Hospital, 20 minutes away. The last thing I remember hearing was my "vitals" taken in the Emergency room - and the last image I saw was you, Gerry.

Did the "walking" pneumonia cause me to hallucinate? Or was it the poignant anniversary of that blessed day so long ago?

I had substituted in High School English earlier, and reminisced frequently about our time with the late Pontiff. No sadness, but instead joy and pride over the event and being there with you.

As the evening wore on, as the sun set, and I drank my malt liquor - a VERY strong one - my mood changed. There was no depression, but rather more reflection on that wonderful day and the memory of you.

I put my cell phone on charge, gradually shut down the computer, and decided to turn in. People say one's life is measured in years, but often ends in just seconds. I stood up, pushed in my computer chair, and felt everything stop.

The terror of suddenly being unable to breathe - and not knowing what I had - is one thing: waking up two days later having lost 36 hours is something else. Then losing another 24 hours, and so it went.

Four days passed before I could communicate with everyone. Using a clipboard, I learned how close I had come to Death myself, although there had not been a "code blue" or "crash cart" call.

I had no memories of anything other than the ambulance, but 18 months later I still wonder if you were there for me Gerry. Were you by my bedside the whole time, watching with those incredible green eyes of yours?

Did you talk to me or touch me? You were the last thing I thought about Gerry, before the attack and as they began the long struggle to save my life. Now, 18 months later, I wonder why I was saved and you were not.

Why was it so necessary for Him to take you, and not let me take care of you instead? Over 20 years of adoring you every time we met, or embracing each stroke of that exquisite, precise handwriting on a postcard or Christmas greeting.

What did you ever do to anyone except try to help their troubled minds?

Update: In the wake of this crisis, I began taking blood pressure medicine and a Vitamin "B" shot. Somehow, doctors missed even then a developing kidney disease, and Easter Week, 2013 I was diagnosed with 3rd stage kidney failure. Three years later, I am one week away from vascular surgery on April 6th, which will enable me to start home dialysis if things steadily worsen.

You went through so much more - and much worse - for so long, Princess.

Am I meant to write this book and make you known to the world? Will I live a long life, write many more articles, and meet another wonderful woman like you? If not, when my time comes to answer our Master's Call, I only ask to spend Eternity wrapped in your arms.

THE ANGEL WORE WHITE - AND PICKED UP THE TAB, TOO.

Once again, Jerry W. recalled something else about you.

"In March of 1992, I was in St. Elizabeth's Hospital for treatment of testicular cancer, undergoing chemotherapy from a bed in the ICU," he began.

"Gerry visited me twice – the first time wearing a white dress – and she also brought some kind of flowers." "I'm terrible about the flowers though, because I think they were White "Mums" - which shows how much I know," he said not long ago.

Unknown to me however, Gerry had been there before herself.

"Some time before this she had been diagnosed with a benign brain tumor, and the doctors had shaved part of her head to operate," said Jerry. So, as the saying goes, "what was past is prologue": you got a taste of what was to eventually come a thousand fold.

"We talked about how things were going in the club and how I was feeling, then after I was discharged she sprang for our lunch twice," said Jerry. We have both marveled at how you were able to keep such a slim figure all the time, Gerry.

" I don't know what she did for exercise, but maybe it was it was her metabolism, because you know how she could really 'wolf' down a meal," said Jerry. Indeed I do, Princess, indeed I do.

All too soon, however - the situation would be reversed.

It would be my new found friend Jerry who would visit YOU in Dayton Hospice. "It became increasingly hard for her to get around," said Jerry. "Kathy and her husband Tom used a van to transport her; she used a walker first then finally a wheelchair - but it became harder and harder to take care of her at home," said Jerry.

I said earlier that seeing my Gerry in a coma was not an option for me. Could I have done so while she was still lucid and somewhat mobile? I don't know. Can any man visit the woman he loves, knowing she's dying?

George Meyer, another CAC ' member,, apparently felt the same way. "George and Gerry had dated in the club, but George said he couldn't bear to see her in a coma, and wouldn't go." Perhaps now, as we Catholics believe, you and George "understand all there is".

18 months ago, as I lay near death from the Pneumonia, George himself passed away. From Cancer. I have come to HATE that word. A LOT.

SUMMER, 1992: ENTER SUPER BITCH: THE ROOM-MATE FROM HELL

There was a period after Kathy got married when you remained behind at Georgetown - perhaps too long. I remember we were talking on the phone one night and you said "paying for this apartment alone is killing my pocketbook - I'm almost broke."

You didn't want a male room-mate, especially any of the guys from CAC, so on and on went the rent. I came to town one week that summer after Gerry had moved in with Roxanne. She owned a house off of Wayne Avenue and my Princess had a room upstairs. How long Gerry had been there I don't know.

BUT, she had warned me, in her super-nice, always kind to everyone way, that "Roxanne just isn't the kind of room-mate one would expect." In other words, as I found out after making plans to pick you up, a real

unfriendly, rude, Lucretia Borgia, bitch. No name change here, either.

She met me at the front door and was, to say the least, surprised.

At what, you might ask? Why, a Black man standing on her porch to pick up this stunning beauty of a tenant, of course. I announced I was there for Gerry, and Roxanne grudgingly - that's with a capital "G" - admitted me. .

"Stand right there," she barked, pointing to an area on her living room rug and making it sound almost like an ultimatum. Gerry came down presently; she wore some type of cream colored or tan outfit - I don't clearly remember - one of her pearl necklaces and a pair of chic high heels.

She gave me a nice hug, and how I wanted to caress her with a vengeance - but we were being watched. She introduced me to Roxanne - who merely glared and grunted - then I suggested we leave.

I walked Gerry to my car and placed her comfortably inside - with Roxanne watching us intently. Perhaps she feared for Gerry's safety, you think? At any rate, we left. Upon our return, I was careful not to give Gerry too long a hug or kiss - because the watch on the Rhine was still going strong. Torn between strangling her and dropping Gerry off, I chose the latter.

20 years later, Roxanne, I still wonder how my Gerry could stand you.

FALL 1992: "I CAN TUCK MYSELF IN JUST FINE; THANK YOU."

My journalism career began in Dayton, but it always flourished elsewhere. A break never materialized there, or in nearby Sidney, Xenia, or even South in Cincinnati or Columbus.

My only job interview with the Dayton Daily News ever came in early September of 1992 - for copy editor along with a test. When I did finally land not one, but two consecutive newspaper jobs, they were in Northern Ohio - away from HER.

For one evening though, several years before, we spent some quality time at the Court Yard Marriott in downtown Dayton. My job interview and test had been earlier in the afternoon, and Gerry knew I would be in town that weekend.

The paper was paying my mileage and putting me up overnight at the hotel. The fly in the ointment: Day Mont -West was being audited or some such rather by the county, or State, or somebody.

Gerry had to work the weekend, getting up Saturday and Sunday bright & early. This meant the octopus in me would have to work fast - if at all.

"We only have time for a couple of drinks, but I'll meet you in the hotel lounge around 7," she had said the day before. When Gerry arrived, I was treated to a stunning new appearance: She had restyled her magnificent, curly brunette locks and some coloring.

It took some getting used to, but I liked the change and told her so. We embraced and I kissed her lightly on the lips - public affection again was not her strong suit. I don't remember now what we ordered, although I remember she liked gin or rum and coke.

I talked about the interview and what a copy editor's duties were, and how nice it would be to see more of her if I got hired. "But what if I were seeing someone,?" she asked - not trying to be cruel or reject me.

"Well, I'm sure we could keep it friendly," I replied, gently massaging her new ringlets with my fingers. There seemed to be something troubling her, what I never did learn - and only now does it come to mind again.

Once again, however, we discovered a common thread that existed between us. Just as she had liked "China Beach" - a reminder of her Red Cross service - she also favored NBC's civil-rights era series "I'll Fly Away."

Yes, we and that "small but loyal following" out there plead guilty after the fact to one charge of helping NBC keep the show on air for two years - at a loss.

For several couples in the lounge that night however, it was "appointment TV" as we now say today. The episode, entitled "Ruler of My Heart", ended with a Black Army officer's murder by three Klansmen in a passing car.

"People need to watch this show," Gerry said quietly afterwards. "They'd learn more about the Civil Right s movement from it than watching any documentary," she added. "I'll Fly Away" concluded, it was time to walk her down to the garage.

I slipped my arm around her perfect waist and held Gerry as tightly as possible. I buried my nose in her newly-minted curls, causing her to giggle softly and say "stop that, Robert." When we reached the garage, I fetched Gerry while a valet fetched the car. Pulling her to me, I kissed her as if my life itself was at stake.

And perhaps it always was. As the valet returned with her car, I released my Princess just a bit. She reached into her tiny clutch purse for the car keys, as I "chewed" gently on her neck and throat. "OK, Robert, OK, it is time for me to go - I Must go," she said. With that, Gerry scooted into the car and closed the door, leaving its window rolled down just ENOUGH. I leaned in quickly and kissed her on the mouth, again.

"Let me follow you home and tuck you in," I said smiling. Gerry looked at me with amused exasperation, and said, "I can tuck myself in, thank you very much." Putting the car in reverse - and rolling up the window to thwart any more moves, she drove off.

The copy editor job, though, did not become mine, and neither did this very special woman. I kept on trying, however, until another rival appeared wanting anything but love. In the end, "He" took everything. Even her.

THE WINTER OF MY DISCONTENT.

From the Kindle book: By MAY, 2013. six months had passed since I began this book .

One day I got a huge offer of help: one of Gerry's co-workers from her mental health job agreed to participate. One more piece in place. A big one. I quickly realized a 100 page book would do the trick nicely.

Now, as March of 2016 ends, I am both nervous and excited. I am incredibly close to realizing something which started at Christmas time as just a mere thought.

I have decided to upload Gerry's book to Amazon as a paperback. Now more than before, I want it to reach the whole world. Gerry deserves this – she did not deserve that horrible thing which befell her.

I said earlier there were only two times when our meetings lacked some of their immense warmth and affection. The second instance was near Christmas, but the 'when' no longer matters.

It was later than many other events I have already recounted, and who knows what was going on in her life at that moment. Maybe she was seriously involved with someone, or perhaps it was an affectionate gesture or thing that I said.

We had coffee in the old Dayton Arcade during its short-lived rebirth, and I told her how my current newspaper job was doing. She seemed uncomfortable and not especially interested, yet when we parted there was no anger between us, or unpleasant looks.

I would not hear from Gerry again for a while, but when I did any recriminations or bad feelings I might have had vanished instantly.

Last month I reached out to two people for their help with this work - and was severely rebuffed.

One person said bluntly that "no one wants to read a memoir", but still I carried on. When really in doubt - I turn once again to my 'second Bible'. - Malamud's "The Fixer", his Pulitzer-Prize winner.

The title character is a quiet, hard-working, and horribly persecuted Jewish handyman. He suffers incredible mistreatment for three years in a Russian prison, falsely accused of a Gentile child's hideous murder. Where he finally goes to trial the book ends - his ultimate fate uncertain - and not even important.

What matters is that he endured - and survived.

Likewise, my Princess fought her injustice for just as long. Yet when I reflect on that moment of awkward parting, I do not hate Gerry. If I did, it would be denying my having loved her so much for so long.

And I will keep on loving her until the end.

4/12/2013: The Day I Became A Kidney Patient

HealthPoint Family Care -Covington Med
1401 Madison Avenue, Covington, KY 41011
(859) 655-6100 Fax: (859) 655-6179

'12/2013 11:54 AM
Page 1 of 2
Referral Form

Referral Form

Authorizing Provider: MD	**Service Provider:** Florence Kidney Disease Consultant
Signing Provider: MD	Kidney Disease Consultant Florence
NPI Number: 1003185679	
Phone: (859) 655-6100	**Phone:** (859) 757-4353
Fax: (859) 655-6186	**Fax:** (859) 534-0865

Patient Name: Robert Glover	**DOB:** 04/28/1953 **Age:** 59
Patient Phone 1: (859) 916-5285	**Sex:** M **SSN:**
Patient Phone 2: () -	
Resp. Provider	**HealthPoint ID #:** 58156

Primary Ins:	ZZ Copay Minimum	Secondary Ins:	
Group:		Group:	
Policy:		Policy:	
Insured:	259949895	Insured ID:	

Code	Description	Diagnoses
KID HTN Referral	Kidney and Hypertension Referral Kidney Disease Consultants Florence	CHRONIC KIDNEY DISEASE STAGE III (MODERATE) (ICD-585.3) HYPERTENSION(ICD-401.9) VITAMIN D DEFICIENCY(ICD-268.9) ANEMIA NOS- B12 DEFICIENCY AND CKD(ICD-285.9)

Order Number:	213169-1		
Auth#:			
Maximum Visits:	99		
Start Date:	04/12/2013	End Date:	03/06/2015
Duration:	99 Weeks		
Reason:	Evaluate & Treat		

Electronically signed by: Rima Desai MD

Signed on: 4/12/2013 11:55:07AM

Patient Address: 336 Chestway Way Apt 106 KY   41071

Newport

Patient Phone #'s: (859) 916-5285   () -

Report run by Rima Desai

JULY 1997: THE HANDWRITING ON MY WALL.

There is nothing special about this chapter - it only concerns a postcard. The card is a brief but lovely one; mailed from Rome, Italy, and written in the most exquisite style on Earth. Look below and see for yourself.

Like the sound of Gerry's voice, and the way she walked, I was hopelessly bewitched by these small, perfectly formed letters and curves which were so much a part of her. I must get more details on that trip.

I know that the entire family went, and that they visited seven countries with London, England part of "our last leg" she wrote me. Gerry loved to travel, and I relish that fact now more than ever; glad that she lived so well.

I wish, however, that we could have traveled together often, but this was not to be. Maybe one day we will; in that perfect place I must believe my Princess has gone to, where she is waiting for me.

The card features some Roman ruins, and Gerry signs off at the end of her report with the words, "see 'ya', - a departure from those two, wonderfully familiar words, "as ever".

.How many postcards did you send to people, and in how many places?

Kathy said your address book had over 300 names in it; I wonder how many of those people will read this book when it is done. No doubt, some of them are persons you met on this trip.

Certainly others belong to that wonderful Saturday we shared in Detroit so long ago. Today is a cold, rainy last Thursday in March. As I work, I remember our adventure, and your untimely end. You are probably wondering why I work on this with pictures of you flanking the computer. Why I keep "YouTube's" window open and play 'Nickelback', Stevie Nicks, 'Journey', 'Enya', and many more titles.

My answer is simple, Princess: the songs keep those feelings of quiet misery at bay that would otherwise destroy me. More questions keep coming to mind, and I write them down, knowing each will generate another chapter.

Where did you do your ballroom dancing? (I remember when you first started it) How much longer would you have worked if IT had not happened? When did you plan to retire - not that fate allowed you to - and what were you going to do after it.?

How was Rome that summer, Princess? No doubt even more lovely with you there. I am sure you revitalized those ruins and their ancient ghosts. Everything and everyone was better for having known you.

Now all I have are memories, and this blessing with words from above.

And I must use this skill – as I have for a lifetime - to honor and remember a dead woman. It – and they – are all I have.
And your handwriting on my wall.

WITH A BODY AND LEGS LIKE THAT, HOW COULD YOU?

Neither Jerry Wildenhaus or I could remember the year this episode took place - only that it was at the CAC Halloween party. What matters now is how unforgettable the whole affair - and you -

remain after more than 15 years.

What am I talking about? Why, you showing up dressed as a 'roaring 20's' flapper. Would anyone have had the willpower to call the police, or would they have even tried to arrest you when they arrived?

Could any of the guys still see straight after viewing you in that outfit? Did you forget your Catholic upbringing for one night? Who cares? It is enough to just picture every jaw-dropping expression that I know must have ensued.

**One Picture REALLY
Is Worth a 1,000 Words.**

"DON'T WORRY, ROBERT; ITS PROBABLY NOTHING."

Cindy Burger Rose sent me several photos, including one of that 'notorious' flapper outfit. She misses you a lot, Gerry, and is always close to tears whenever we talk. Cindy believes you had a good reason for not telling me you were sick - and then later that you were dying.

"It's a hard thing to tell someone that you're dying - and Gerry wasn't the kind of person to burden someone else with her illness," said Cindy.

When her battle began however, I still lived in Michigan. Then a marvelous writing opportunity with the Cincinnati and Kentucky POST newspapers put me just an Hour away from her. At the wrong time. And, although I reached out to Gerry several times after getting settled, that conversation – ending with those words which I now know were a lie even as she spoke them,, proved to be our last one.

I became the 'odd man out' -a distinction that carries with it no pleasure whatsoever - only pain.

THINGS THOSE LEFT BEHIND MUST DO: THEY ALL STINK.

When a much beloved person dies, there are always those left behind. They are known as the survivors. And there are things they must do.

In March, 2003, the Cincinnati POST ran a feature by me entitled "The Survivors". It concerned bereavement support groups. Little did I know how much it would concern me one day.

In Gerry's case - as it was in my mother's bedroom after her passing - there were the old medicine bottles to throw out. I know now that there were a lot of them, because she was in so much pain. Her last letter to everyone, which - she said "took me almost three months to write, even with help", had to be mailed out.

Despite its downbeat subject, This remains one of my favorite POST articles.

A car she could no longer drive, perhaps months before Hospice, disposed of or passed on to others. We must choose between attending the viewing, the funeral, or doing both. Eventually, the apartment will be cleaned up and emptied out - when others are finally strong enough to do it.

The utility company will turn off the lights. One day, some of us will revisit his grave or hers - to grieve, remember, and lessen our pain. And, whether it concerns Gerry, my mother, or someone else, the whole thing stinks. Because now , WE are "The Survivors".

THERE'S NO SUCH THING AS 'FEELING A PRESENCE'. IS THERE?

October 6th, 2011: It is just after 6 p.m., and getting dark outside.

Our Detroit Tigers are playing the Texas Rangers in a playoff game, and have a good shot at going to the World Series. As the 4th inning ends, I go to my bedroom to put up classroom attire I worked in that day.

I turn on a night stand lamp - and enter The Twilight Zone. Where did that incredibly powerful smell of perfume come from? I did not imagine it; having walked past enough cosmetic counters in department stores to recognize the scent.

No, I did not see HER upon looking around - but wish I had. I was one week out of the hospital, and Gerry was not on my mind that evening. Just baseball, and taking my post ICU/pneumonia medication.

I still wonder 'where' she had been - sitting on my bed, or beside me the whole time? Had she decided to leave a calling card? Gerry's friend Cindy Rose, who took over Gerry's apartment after she died, thinks so.

"I spent that horrible, first Christmas after she passed away in it, and I definitely felt a presence," said Cindy. "Perhaps it was because I was around all her things, or maybe it was because she was really there," said Cindy.

I want to believe that she was around, too - both Cindy and myself.

The trouble is, those we miss with our heart and soul never show themselves - but how would I react if Gerry did? Would it be too much for this broken heart to bear when she disappears?

They come when they want, go when they want, and worry about nothing in between. Does she know how much I miss her, or how the slightest mention of her suffering by Cindy made me well up?

"She wanted to eat 'Frisches' one night at Hospice but eventually couldn't because her stomach hurt so much," said Cindy. "She was in so much pain that night, and asked me to spend the night, so I did."

I carried this painful footnote around with me for a while, then later, while watching an episode of "Blue Bloods", I broke down. Sometimes one piece of information hurts worse than any memory.

In the end, however, we still wind up talking to - and hurting - by ourselves.

A RETIREMENT NEVER REACHED, TRIPS NEVER TAKEN

I remember when these photos were first emailed to me.

They are from Gerry's former employer Day Mont-West, a Mental Health Clinic in Dayton, Ohio. I look at them and I am happy because they show off her beauty, poise and humanity.

I am also sad because I missed so much of her life. Like a serviceman or woman posted abroad, I missed her birthdays, and never saw her ballroom dance. I did see her grow more beautiful every year- through those visits I will treasure forever.

I remember seeing that new, highlighted hairstyle seen in her 20th anniversary service photo, because it was our last time together. I am glad she could pose for the picture with her 25th year of service gold watch; glad she could still walk.

I can see the difference in Gerry's face, and how her body has changed,, from those many operations and treatments. I can tell she has endured a lot - and I know she is wearing a wig. On another note, we change as we get older, though, and I wonder if I might have never won Gerry over completely enough to wed.

That would have been fine too; anything with her would have been better than what I have now - memories and this book. Look at the two earlier photos if you will: check out those exquisite eyes, that lovely hair, the way she stands so tall, perfect and straight.

Behold that magnificent body, filled with warmth and softness. Just holding her in one's arms as we greeted each other during a visit was total paradise. Yet I cannot look at the photo of her fashion show bridesmaid without regretting once again that she never married.

And one other thing still needs no prompting for me to recall it.

I have heard the sound of her voice so well these past few days: the precise way she always spoke, that slight movement of her head. "She was just so feminine in the way she walked and moved," said Gaynell Durham, one of Gerry's supervisors at Day-Mont Behavioral Health Care.

"It was the grace in her - the kind of social skills she had," recalled Gaynell, who spoke about Gerry's kindness after two other co-workers had passed away earlier. "Gerry went to each and every family member at both viewings, speaking to them, holding their hands, comforting them, after other people had either taken their seats or left," said Gaynell.

As I look at Gerry posing with her 25th year service pin, the subtle changes in her are noticeable. The sparkle is still there in that gentle smile - but somehow everything is different. Picturing her marvelous, highlighted hair turned grey from the "chemo" is difficult, - just like knowing now that she would be gone in a few months.

"I continued working until my illness made it impossible," said Gerry in her final letter. I asked Gaynell what Gerry's last day at Day-Mont was like - but the answer was not what I expected. You see, I had imagined a day where her co-workers would say good-bye, perhaps give her a present or two, some hugs, and wish her well. Not so.

"Gerry had been off work for a while, and the day she came back, she got really sick," said Gaynell. "We knew that she was ill, but not how serious it was, and since everyone worked in cubicles, we all kept an eye on her." In the end, a Day-Mont staffer took my Gerry home - "I still remember it like it was yesterday said Gaynell, "and the next time we heard from her, she was in (Dayton) Hospice."

Gerry asked Gaynell to come visit her her, "but I couldn't do it although other people here did go," recalled Gaynell. How long would she have remained at Day-Mont had not fate struck her down? "We talked about it once or twice some time before she got sick, and I remember her saying she would like to work somewhere else," said Jerry Wildenhaus.

Gaynell agreed, noting that "she probably would have moved on someplace other than Day-Mont." We will never know for certain - just as I will always wonder why His plan for her did not involve me staying in her life. No opportunity to remain her friend, or reaffirm my love for her.

Not everyone will like hearing such feelings, but I stopped worrying about that long ago. In mid-April, I may have to begin peritoneal dialysis at home, three years after first being diagnosed with third stage kidney disease.

It was labeled 'moderate and treatable' at the time, and the medical term is "nephritis". I will be damned by some if I finish this - and by myself if I don't. This will NOT happen.

Another one of Gerry's co- worker's - I call her 'Sandy', - was "hesitant" to talk with me about visiting Gerry in Hospice. The pain is as fresh today as it was then. Is Sandy black or white?

In the end, it does not make any difference. Because, you see, both of us still love her.

My Princess as The Image of Perfection. Poised, Polite, and Beautiful Beyond Words.

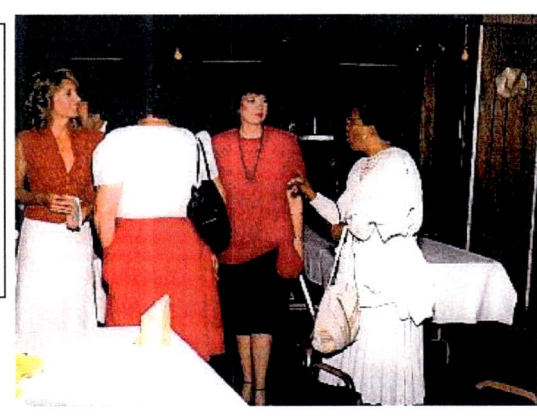

Gerry As A Bridesmaid in One of Daymont-West's Early Fashion Shows.

THE LAST DANCE: I WISH SHE COULD HAVE - WE ALL DO.

I always knew how I wanted to end this book. I always believed that The event I now described had to be placed here. And I knew the pain that doing so would cause me. Labor Day weekend, 2013, I paid the forfeit.

The annual CAC Christmas Dinner Dance has always been a huge event - and was an important one for Gerry. Yet, while her last letter tells us how much she enjoyed it - did she know this might be her last one?

Six weeks before, in mid-November, she walked down the aisle at her baby sister Margo's wedding - assisted by brother in-law Tom. Now, even though I know she was on a walker by then, I must ask myself the painful question: what was THIS dinner-dance like for her?

"The dance was held at the Christopher Club, and Gerry was driven there by Kathy and her brother in-law Tom," said Jerry Wildenhaus. Kathy stayed, and they had brought Gerry's wheelchair and her walker," he recalled.

"I walked around the dance floor, and Gerry sat talking with talking with a lot of her friends," he continued. Gerry always loved the Christmas Dinner-Dance, but now the Time had come when she could not dance at all.

"I don't think she would have been able to dance, even if she wanted to, and I remember she wore a sort of red-colored dress, because women like to wear red at Christmas time," said Jerry.

The Christmas dinner dance ended, winter came and went, but as Gerry's farewell poem 'Folks' said, "once again my cards weren't sent." Too weak to handle this task, she kept hoping for a miracle nonetheless. "I talked to her on the phone once when she was in Hospice, and we discussed the CAC convention coming up in San Antonio," said Jerry.

"I would really like to try and go to that," she said, but was worried about her appearance. "I probably look like I just left a concentration camp, I've lost so much weight." Gerry did not go to San Antonio, and I paid the price of this new-found knowledge, continually snapping the cap of my Paper-Mate pen on and off, throwing it down after writing his comments, then picking it up again.

I found out what I wanted to know, and now must pass it on to others. Soon I must go to Dayton again, and visit the Hospice to drop off this paperback edition. I also want to take pictures of the pond, its waterfall, and the ducks. I will try to avoid looking at the window which marks her old room. I will struggle to bar the words "wheelchair" and "walker" from my mind.

It was Gerry's last CAC Christmas Dinner Dance, and she couldn't even manage a slow one.

I am currently in Hospice. I don't know if I will have the opportunity to write you again. It is hard to know what to say to all of you, except that I am thankful to have had you in my life. Please keep me In your prayers, as I believe that with God's grace, miracles do happen. My love to all of you." Gerry.

FOR WHOM DOES THE BELL TOLL? WHY, ME OF COURSE.

Upon returning from Dayton on April 4, I promptly kept a routine, already scheduled doctor's appointment in nearby Bellevue. Locating a primary care doctor had been difficult after my move.

When I did find one - and qualified as a 'self-pay' (see no insurance and low income) - a backlog of flu cases post phoned my first visit. A routine blood draw brought me back to the doctor several days later.

She repeated the lab work – producing the same results - and then came the diagnosis. I had an abnormally large loss of protein, due to a filtration problem. The issue is called "FSGS" - its medical term shortened - scarring of the nephrons. These modules inside my kidneys are damaged, and the pneumonia shrunk them slightly.

No, dialysis won't be necessary; nor is kidney failure on the horizon or even a transplant. We start with one more generic prescription - a steroid called "Lycinopryl" - and I go back to my doctor in a month.

I thought starting this entry would be difficult, that I would struggle with words and thoughts. Instead, an entire page took shape in a flash. How could I not see by now how important - and how easy - this whole thing is to do? Am I working alone, or is someone spurring me on?

Once again, I must ask the question - why have I been spared at least once - and now face a crisis that at least holds some hope? Gerry was forever hopeful until there was no hope.

"She was determined to beat it," said her sister Kathy. Until 'IT', decided to take no prisoners. Am I under pressure now to finish this book? Hardly. I just have a responsibility to finish it: for Gerry, her mother, her male friend Jerry – who has helped me so much - and GOD.

All others need not apply, so take heed and don't bother me. I return to it now more determined than ever - and with an insight into what my beloved must have gone through time and time again.

First there was the mystery pain, followed by that first diagnosis, then all those waits for more test results. There were the endless series of operations, a parade of prescriptions, agony and private despair.

"I know she cried a lot," said Kathy as we left Calvary after my first visit. "There were times when she would answer the phone or the door when she was off work - and many times she would not," said Jerry. The more I learn, the more I grieve - because an Interstate and not knowing Gerry's situation kept me from her.

"I have no doubt that, had you known, you would have been there the same day," my pastor had said. After the 25th anniversary event, there were two more rounds of 'chemo', and her baby sister Margo's wedding. Then another trip to the Cancer Center in Houston, A stay at Kathy's, a room at Dayton Hospice, and she was gone.

When visiting the KROGER pharmacy for my $600.00 worth of "scripts", (now nothing, due to Obamacare on January 1st), or checking my blood pressure on its machine, I realize how lucky I am: my prognosis is pretty good: even with the nephritis being hereditary.

If no good deed does go unpunished, is this my punishment for loving Gerry? Only time, and treatment, will tell. Like my Princess, I can only wait.

IN MY OWN WORDS.

I am an Air Force "brat", raised across the U. S. and overseas in Spain and Japan. I took First Communion in Spanish and English at a Castilian Cathedral in Madrid. Japan exposed our family to civil unrest, and two consecutive, terrible earthquakes.

Georgia baptized me in the ways of post-Civil Rights era prejudices, yet I became a tolerant, liberal, double-edged sword. The University of Dayton gave me a college education, and three years on The Flyer News an extra career I never imagined.

Four books I keep by my bedside personify me best.. A copy of the New Testament, speeches by Dr. Martin Luther King, Jr., Mahatma Gandhi's autobiography "This Life", and the now totally forgotten Jewish author Bernard Malamud's 1966, Pulitzer - Prize winning novel, "The Fixer."

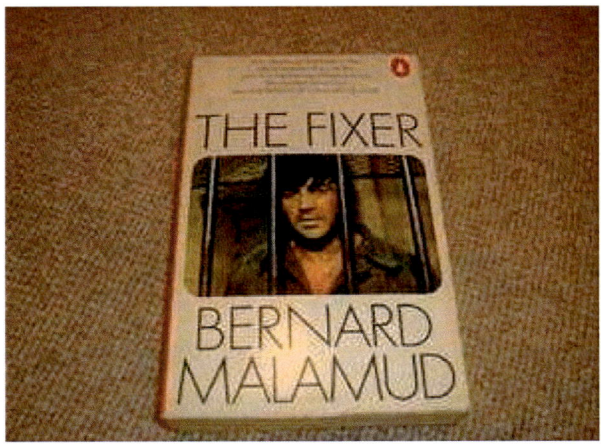

"I have committed no crime, I need no pardon." I want a trial; you called me criminal, now you must prove it."

These four books - especially "The Fixer" - guided me through an extremely negative time at U. of D. Racial separatism was rampant on campus then - much of it caused by Black on Black "reverse racism", pure and simple.

The idea of separating us from the White students was promoted by a group called "B.A. T. U.", or "Black Action Through Unity". What, among other things, upset them so much?

"If they didn't run a photo of you with that damned movie column, people would think you were White,' said their ringleader. Intimidation, enormous acrimony, bullying, threats, and periodic physical violence,

I survived it all. I never changed schools for fear of ending my newly found, accidental career. Now I must hope to achieve more milestones like those earlier ones, but without Gerry.

Over the years I developed discipline, persistence, and endured incredible adversity as many people opposed both me and my "mainstream" writing style. Remember, dear readers, that Louis Farrakhan himself decreed " any Black journalist who writes for the "White Devil" is damned." Even these words are connected to what I write and my beautiful Gerry.

She never spoke a single comment about race to anyone who knew her. Including me. She never got upset with anyone, was very methodical, treated every person she met the same. As a fellow Catholic, was true to our Faith unto Death.

No doubt many people will dismiss these words, or just say "he had a thing for this white woman". Yes, I did — and still do. Yet the truth is something entirely different. Because this book, like Gerry herself, is decent and honest. Within these pages are the contents of my heart. Like my first visit to Gerry's grave, it is something I have to do.

EPILOG: THE EASIEST AND HARDEST THING I EVER WROTE.

Today is March 31st, 2016.

My Kindle e-book will soon be replaced by this paperback, probably 100 pages in length, sometime in April. It was on Kindle for two years, with acceptable sales. Now, once again, the story of my love for Gerry is done.

Today I compiled a list of people whom I think will appreciate receiving a copy of it. In March, 2014, Kathy refused to accept the book or even consider reading it. Silence and some very unkind words from her husband, Tom, were my reward for writing this book.

Today I saw a vascular surgeon and nurse at St. Elizabeth's Hospital in Edgewood, Kentucky. Next Wednesday, April 6th, at 10 a.m., I will undergo surgery to insert a catheter for possible, future home dialysis.

Mother Nature has been most kind to me, these past three years, but the miracle that eluded my Princess has apparently escaped me, too.

Since May, 2014, I lector once a month at St. Henry's Catholic Church in Erlanger. A neighbor will drive me to St. E's and wait downstairs until the one hour 'procedure' is done. A stomach hernia is being treated, too.

I try to avoid thinking of all the suffering that Gerry endured, the physical deterioration, weakness, or the terrible pain she was in. Then the coma she slipped into before she died.

Things have finally started to improve with my finding writing work. I am a regular in the Tennessee TRIBUNE, Nashville's highly

respected, 25 year-old African American weekly. And as Jerry said, "
don't forget, you wrote a book, didn't you?"

A long life was not in the cards for Gerry - nor was a life with
me or - it seems now - any other man. We all lost her - but how many
who knew my Princess still grieve for her like I do?

I realize now that she spared me her ordeal in Hospice; I
believe it would have killed me. How long I will be on dialysis is
unknown, and things can always get better. Whether I will need a
transplant or not is equally uncertain. I am on the list for one, however,
at the University of Louisville.

Why did she have to suffer so much for so long, when all I
have experienced is worry? A 'ground rule' of every grief support group
is the one which says "your grief is unique and therefore not open to
comparison."

Likewise, neither is my grief open to apologies for having
loved - and still being in love with - this woman. These pages are all the
proof that I - or anyone else - should need. If my affection for
Geraldine Lee Fish is a 'crime', then its penalty – if there is one –
cannot be pronounced upon me by anyone in this life.

ROBERT ALAN GLOVER. MARCH 31ST, 2016, SEPT. 24, 2013

I'M THERE INSIDE YOUR HEART

Right now I'm in a different place And though we seem apart, I'm closer than I ever was, I'm there inside your heart.

I'm with you when you greet each day And while the sun shines bright, I'm there to share the sunsets, too I'm with you every night.

I'm with you when the times are good, To share a laugh or two, And if a tear does start to fall, I'll still be there for you. And when that day arrives, that we are no longer apart, I'll smile and hold you close to me. Forever in my heart.

FUNERAL PRAYER: SAYING GOOD BYE TO A PRINCESS.

Family and Friends, For those of you that do not know me, my name is Greg Wood. I am here speaking to you because a number of years ago Gerry asked me to say something nice about her at her funeral should she precede me in death.

It is very easy to say nice things about Gerry. She was one of the most kind, giving and thoughtful people I have ever met. She never forgot a birthday or some special occasion and she always provided little gifts of love to show how much she cared for those she loved.

As a social worker she also showed her kind, giving and loving nature in working with the elderly. Gerry was a very loving person. Gerry was also a very strong and courageous woman. She battled a most hideous disease through many operations and hospital stays and she never lost her will to live or her zest for life.

I met Gerry 35 years ago in front of the cafeteria at Wright State University. I didn't know at the time that my life would never be the same again. Through that meeting I gained another family that I consider as much a family to me as my own family. For that I cannot thank Gerry enough.

While this is indeed a sad time as we to say good by to Gerry Fish, I want to look at it as a time that we are saying good by to someone moving to a new place, one that is so much better that their old home.

We are sad to see them go as we say our good byes, for we will dearly miss them, but as they reach their new home there is another gathering of loved ones waiting to say "Welcome." I will mention three.

I see "Pa" Fish there saying "Welcome Gerry Lee. Let me show you my place here, it is wonderful. My garage is so big I can't fill it up." "Welcome."

I see my Mother, Mary saying " Welcome Gerry. You look so pretty. Let me show you where we dance here. I know you love to dance, and here you never get tired." "Welcome."

Finally, I see Julie Arquilla there saying "Welcome Gerry. Let's go for a walk. I just want to show you how beautiful it is here, the flowers are so lovely and there are no weeds." "Welcome." As I say good bye to Gerry, I know that when it is my turn to move to a new place, that you will be there to say, "Welcome."

A LOVE REMEMBERED IS A LOVE FOREVER
ONE MAN'S TRIBUTE TO A WOMAN HE CANNOT FORGET
BY ROBERT ALAN GLOVER

Gerry Fish (L.) with close friend Rose Carone.
Event Was Most Likely A CAC Convention;
Date Sometime In the 1980's.

Made in the USA
San Bernardino, CA
23 October 2016